SO-CDL-117

THE BIG BOOK OF DAD JOKES

Dear Dad,

_____

_____

_____

_____

_____

Copyright © 2020

All rights reserved. No part of this publication may be reproduced, distributed, or transmitted in any form or by any means, including photocopying, recording, or other electronic or mechanical methods, without the prior written permission of the publisher, except in the case of brief quotations embodied in critical reviews and certain other noncommercial uses permitted by copyright law. For permission requests, contact the publisher.

**A man has been stealing
wheels off of police cars.**

Police are working
tirelessly to catch him.

**As a lumberjack, I know that
I've cut exactly 2,417 trees.**

I know because every time
I cut one, I keep a log.

**Want to hear a joke
about a piece of paper?**

Never mind...it's tearable.

You heard of that new band 999-Megabytes?

They're good but they haven't got a gig yet.

I told my 14 year old son I thought 'Fortnite' was a stupid name for a computer game.

I think it's just two week.

I accidentally booked myself onto an escapology course.

I'm really struggling to get out of it.

I watched a dwarf escape from prison by climbing down a fence.

I thought to myself, "That's a little condescending."

Every time I take pictures of wheat fields . . .

They always come out grainy.

My wife thinks I'm addicted to brake fluid.

I keep telling her I could stop at any time.

What's the difference between ignorance and apathy?

I don't know and I don't care.

Telling your suitcase there's no vacation this year can be tough.

Emotional baggage is the worst.

Have you noticed we never hear about grave robbers nowadays?

Apparently it's a dying art.

How do you make holy water?

You boil the hell out of it.

Did you know the first French fries weren't actually cooked in France?

They were cooked in Greece.

If a child refuses to sleep during nap time, are they guilty of resisting a rest?

My wife is really mad at the fact that I have no sense of direction.

So I packed up my stuff and right.

I'm reading a book about anti-gravity.

It's impossible to put down.

I ordered a chicken and an egg online.

I'll let you know.

A slice of apple pie is $2.50 in Jamaica and $3.00 in the Bahamas.

These are the pie rates of the Caribbean.

If you see a robbery at an Apple Store . . .

. . . does that make you an iWitness?

Don't trust atoms.

They make up everything.

Why did the invisible man turn down the job offer?

He couldn't see himself doing it.

What's the best part about living in Switzerland?

I don't know, but the flag is a big plus.

Why couldn't the bike standup by itself?

It was two tired.

What do you call a deer with no eyes?

No idea.

I used to have a job at a calendar factory but I got the sack because I took a couple of days off.

A ham sandwich walks into a bar and orders a beer.

The bartender says, "Sorry, we don't serve food here."

What did the buffalo say to his son when he dropped him off at school?

Bison.

Why did the crab never share?

Because he's shellfish.

Two peanuts were walking down the street.

One was a salted.

Why couldn't the mail person delivery any envelopes?

They were stationary.

What do ghosts serve for dessert?

I scream.

I was going to tell a vegetable joke.

But it's corny.

**What is the loudest
pet you can get?**

A trumpet.

**What do you call a
factory that sells
passable products?**

A satisfactory.

**Did you hear about
the circus fire?**

It was in tents!

I was interrogated over the theft of a cheese toastie.

Man, they really grilled me.

If you rearrange the letters of "Postmen".

They get really annoyed.

I had a dream that I was a muffler last night.

I woke up exhausted!

A cowboy asked me if I could help him round up 18 cows.

I said, 'Yes, of course - that's 20 cows'.

I'm entering the world's tightest hat competition.

Just hope I can pull it off

I usually meet my wife at 12:59.

I like that one-to-one time.

I never lie on my resume.

Because it creases it.

**If you're being chased by
a pack of taxidermists,
do not play dead.**

**I've been happily
married for four years.**

Out of a total of 10.

I'm rubbish with names. It's not my fault, it's a condition. There's a name for it...

I like to imagine the guy who invented the umbrella was going to call it the 'brella'. But he hesitated.

As a kid I was made to walk the plank.

We couldn't afford a dog.

Crime in multi-storey car parks.

That is wrong on so many different levels.

I saw a documentary on how ships are kept together.

Riveting.

I've been diagnosed with a terrible disease that makes me tell airport jokes.

The doctor says it's terminal.

**My friend suggesting
buying a telescope.**

I'm looking into it.

I don't trust stairs.

They're always
up to something.

**Before the crowbar
was invented . . .**

Most crows drank at home.

I have a lot of unemployment jokes.

But none of them work.

If I disappeared into the fog tomorrow . . .

Would I be mist?

Why do so many spiders work in IT?

They're great web-developers.

I didn't like my beard before.

But lately, it's been
growing on me.

**Someone stole my
dictionary and thesaurus.**

I don't know what to say,
I have no words.

**Doctor: Sorry for
being late.**

Man: It's not a
problem, I'm patient.

A midget that could speak to the dead escaped from prison.

The news reported on the small medium at large.

Two Goldfish in a tank.

One says to the other, "Do you know how to drive this thing?"

Two antennas on a roof fell in love and got married.

The wedding wasn't much. But the reception was incredible.

**I just read a book about
the history of glue.**

I couldn't put it down.

Why did the baker go to work?

He kneads the dough.

**How many countries
border Germany?**

Nein.

Two jumper cables walk into a bar.

The bartender says, "I'll serve you, but don't start anything."

Did you hear about the farmer who won an award for his dedication to his crops?

He was out standing in his field.

My daughter thinks I'm overprotective and nosy.

At least that's what she wrote in her diary.

**The other day I yelled
into a colander.**

My voice was strained.

**Someone threw a
bottle of mayo at me.**

I was like what the Helman!

**My son told me, "The car manual
says that I shouldn't turn up the
stereo to full volume."**

I said, "That's sound advice."

I tried to come up with a joke about social distancing.

But this is as close as I could get.

How do depressed frogs die?

They Kermit suicide.

To whoever stole my copy of Microsoft Office . . .

I will find you. You have my Word.

**I can cut down a tree
only using my vision.**

I saw it with my own eyes.

**My daughter said she didn't
want to deal with lice.**

But I told her we had to
tackle this problem head on.

**I own the world's
worst thesaurus.**

Not only is it awful...But it's awful.

Electrons have mass?

I didn't even know
they were Catholic.

**My Grandma is 96 years old and
she still doesn't need glasses.**

She drinks straight from the bottle.

**Did you hear about the
restaurant on the moon?**

Great food, no atmosphere.

My wife asked me, "Do you think our kids are spoiled?"

I said, "No. Most of them smell that way."

What do you call two monkeys that share an Amazon account?

Prime mates.

How does Moses make coffee?

He-brews it.

I don't have a "Dad Bod".

I have a father figure.

**Why do North Koreans
draw the straightest lines?**

Because they have
a supreme ruler.

**I was going to buy the world's most
haunted house. I toured it, but it
seemed like a normal house.**

Nothing jumped out at me.

I could have been an astronaut.

But my parents told me
the sky was the limit.

I prefer dad jokes about eyes.

The cornea the better.

**What kind of flour do
you buy an orphan.**

Self-raising flour.

My son asked if I could tell him what a solar eclipse is.

I said "No sun".

What's the best time of day?

6:30 hands down.

All of my mom's sisters are incredibly healthy.

Thanks to all of their auntie-bodies.

My friend said he broke his tibia. Upon examining his X-rays, I can tell he lied.

It was a fibula.

What do you call a cave man who takes forever to get anywhere?

A meanderthal.

Did you hear about the lay-offs aboard the haunted pirate ship?

They're down to a skeleton crew.

What do women and grenades have in common?

Once you pull off the ring your house is gone.

Why is there no COVID-19 in Antarctica?

Because they are in ice-olation.

I just found out I'm colorblind.

The diagnosis came completely out of the purple.

**What type of snake is
best at arithmetic?**

An adder.

You need help with an Ark?

Don't worry, I Noah guy.

**I told my wife she was drawing
her eyebrows too high.**

She looked surprised.

I wrote a song about a tortilla.

Actually, it's more of a wrap.

**Stephen King has
a son named Joe.**

I'm not joking – but he is.

Our wedding was so emotional.

Even the cake was in tiers.

What type of fruit is not allowed to get married?

Cantaloupe.

My dad's answer to everything is alcohol.

He doesn't drink, he's just terrible at crosswords.

Einstein finally finished his space theory.

It's about time.

Why can't you trust anything balloons say?

They're full of hot air.

How many tickles does it take to make an octopus laugh?

Ten tickles.

I just got attacked by a gang of mime artists.

They did unspeakable things to me.

**I'm having trouble organising
a hide-and-seek league.**

Good players are hard to find.

**Why can't the bank
keep a secret?**

It has too many tellers.

Why are ghosts such bad liars?

You can see right through them.

**Where did Noah keep
a record of his bees?**

In the ark hives.

**I woke up this morning and found
that someone has dumped a
bunch of celery on my front porch.**

I think I'm being stalked.

**My dad didn't love me as a child,
but I don't really blame him.**

I wasn't born until he was an adult.

Why did the man driving the train get struck by lightning?

He was a good conductor.

Why does the letter J always have to run?

Because jaywalking is illegal.

Someone stole all the toilet seats at the police station.

The police are trying to find the thief but they have nothing to go on.

My daughter was involved in a peekaboo related injury.

She's currently in the I.C.U.

My wife bet me a 1,000 bucks that I couldn't build a car out of noodles.

You should have seen the look on her face as I drove pasta.

I walked into a bank, pointed a long, thin piece of wood at the ceiling and shouted . . .

This is a stick up!

A man was found guilty as charged in a lawsuit filed by Netflix.

It was after a 30-day trial.

A courtroom artist was arrested today.

The details are sketchy.

I wondered why the frisbee was getting bigger.

Then it hit me.

I recently heard about a mannequin that lost all of his friends.

He was too clothes minded.

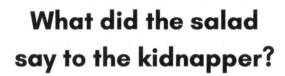

What did the salad say to the kidnapper?

Lettuce go.

I love to tell dad jokes.

Sometimes he even laughs.

What does an Englishman say when he wants to know how you're doing?

UK?

Why did the dolphins elect a dictator?

Because they wanted to serve a greater porpoise.

What do you call bears without ears?

B

**My wife warned me not
to steal kitchen utensils.**

But it's a whisk I'm willing to take.

**Very few people know about
the first ever female vegan.**

Nobody has heard of herbivore.

**Did you hear about the guy who
invented the knock-knock joke?**

He won the Nobel Prize.

What do you call illegal, fermented milk?

Mooshine.

What do you call a can opener that doesn't work?

A can't opener.

What kind of training do you need to become a garbage collector?

None, you just pick it up as you go along.

Welcome to plastic surgery addicts anonymous.

I see a few new faces here this week.

If I don't perfect human cloning . . .

I won't be able to live with myself.

Why is camping such a rush?

Because it's in-tents.

I can't buy beer since I started working in the coal mine.

They don't sell alcohol to miners.

What's a pirate's favorite letter.

P - without it they're irate.

Why did the chicken cross the road?

Social distancing.

**Can a kangaroo jump
higher than a house?**

Of course, houses can't jump.

What is a boxer's favorite drink?

Punch.

**Some people in my town were
protesting by transplanting
the courthouse lawn.**

It was a grassroots movement.

What did 17 say to 34?

I'm in my prime.

How do you make a tissue dance?

You put a little boogie in it.

How do locomotives hear?

Through their engineers.

My appointment was cancelled.

It was a dis-appointment.

'I'm arresting you for illegally downloading Wikipedia!'

'Wait! I can explain everything!'

I was cold while in my kayak so I lit a fire and it sunk.

Shows you can't have your kayak and heat it too.

I nearly missed the marathon yesterday.

I was running late.

Dogs can't operate MRI machines.

But catscan.

What sound does a bullet shot in church make?

Pew pew pew.

If you don't succeed the first time . . .

Maybe parachuting isn't for you.

Where do sharks go on vacation?

Finland.

**How do crazy people
go through the forest?**

They take the psycho path.

Some children treat their parents like god.

They act like they don't exist until they want something.

Did you hear the rumor about butter?

Well, I'm not going to spread it.

Someone at work stole my Nikes and my high-viz vest.

They can run but they cannot hide.

**My neighbor denies
throwing a cinder block
through my front window.**

But I have concrete evidence.

**On my wedding day I want someone
to pour hot water on my legs.**

So I don't get cold feet.

**My friend was diagnosed
with water on the brain.**

We gave him a tap on the
head and he's fine now.

Why are double amputations so expensive?

They cost an arm and a leg.

My wife told me we didn't need the surround system I bought for our living room.

I told her it was a sound investment.

George Washington predicted that some day a dollar bill will contain his likeness.

He was on the money.

I had a really good job at
the park sweeping leaves.

I was just raking it in.

I am a little confused about
why everyone keeps giving
me legos for my birthday.

I don't know what to make of it.

What do you call a
retired boxer who loves
to play video games?

Xbox-er.

My house was broken into last night. They took my dictionary and my scrabble board.

I'm lost for words.

My wife was up until 2am pretending to be an absorbent cloth.

She's a real night towel.

Yesterday, I crossed the road, changed a light bulb and walked into a bar.

My life is turning into a joke.

**If you ever get jumped by
a gang of clowns . . .**

Go for the juggler.

What do you call a wandering nun?

A roamin Catholic.

**Why did the Thai pepper
put on a jacket?**

Because it was a little chili.

I heard a dwarf got pickpocketed. I was shocked and appalled.

How could anyone stoop so low.

What if I lifted a pack of Coca-Cola over my head for twenty minutes a day every day?

That would be soda pressing.

Did you hear about the two men who were arrested for stealing a calendar?

They each got six months.

I like my dentist so much . . .

I gave him a little plaque.

What do you call a hippy's wife?

Mississippi.

**What do you call a
cow with no legs?**

Ground beef.

What's so good about Soviet Ubers?

They're always Russian.

Where do nerdy astronauts hang out?

The dork side of the moon.

What kind of horse comes out at night?

A nightmare.

**Why was it so hot
in the Apple store?**

Because they don't
support windows.

**What did Catwoman say
after kidnapping Santa?**

This cat's got Claus.

**I once knew an Irish man who
could bounce off walls.**

His name was Rick O'Shea.

Why don't atheists weigh anything?

Because they have no mass.

Want to hear something funny?

Quarantine, actually you wouldn't understand, it's an inside joke.

Eating a clock is very time-consuming.

Conjunctivitis.com

Now that's a site for sore eyes.

What happens when a panda escapes a zoo?

It causes panda-monuim.

Have you heard the music of Pelvis Presley?

He's hip.

How do you cut
an ocean in half?

With a sea-saw.

The invention of the shovel . . .

Was groundbreaking.

If I had to rate our solar
system, I'd give it one star.

Did you know you can always find Will Smith in the snow?

Just follow the fresh prints.

Why did Mozart get rid of his old songs after he died?

Because he was decomposing.

I'm so poor, I can't even pay attention.

**Why didn't the golfer play
in the PGA tournament?**

He wasn't feeling up to par.

I hate Russian dolls.

They're so full of themselves.

**Earth is the third planet
from the sun.**

This means all our problems
are third-world problems.

I once tried to invent a belt made of wristwatches.

It turned out to be a waist of time.

I was thinking of running a marathon, but I think it might be too difficult getting all the roads closed and providing enough water for everyone.

I'm going to donate my body to science, and keep my Dad happy – he always wanted me to go to medical school.

**My grandfather invented
the cold air balloon.**

But it never really took off.

**My New Year's resolution
is to get in shape.**

I choose round.

**My Dad used to say
'fight fire with fire'.**

Which is probably why he got
thrown out of the fire brigade.

What do sprinters eat before a race?

Nothing, they fast.

What happens when you go to the bathroom in France?

European.

Want to hear a joke about construction?

I'm still working on it.

**I used to work in a
shoe-recycling shop.**

It was sole destroying.

**My boss told me to
have a good day.**

So I went home.

I'm so good at sleeping.

I can do it with
my eyes closed.

Spring is here!

I got so excited I wet my plants.

This graveyard looks overcrowded.

People must be dying to get in.

Did you hear about the Italian chef who died?

He pasta way.

What's ET short for?

Because he's only got tiny legs.

**I don't play soccer because
I enjoy the sport.**

I'm just doing it for kicks.

**What do you call a donkey
with only three legs?**

A wonkey.

What do Santa's elves listen to as they work?

Wrap music.

I think my wife is putting glue on my antique weapons collection.

She denies it but I'm sticking to my guns.

Why do trees seem suspicious on sunny days?

They just seem a little shady.

Last night I dreamt that I weighed less than a thousandth of a gram.

I was like, 0mg.

A cheese factory exploded in France.

Da brie is everywhere.

I've been bored recently so I've taken up fencing.

The neighbors said they will call the police unless I put it back.

I don't attend funerals
that start before noon.

I guess I'm just not a
mourning person.

If two vegans get in a fight,
is it still considered a beef?

One of my favorite memories
as a kid was when my
brothers used to put me
inside a tire and roll me down
a hill. They were Goodyears.

What musical instrument is found in the bathroom?

A tuba toothpaste.

I dreamt about drowning in an ocean of orange soda.

It was just a Fanta-sea.

What are the strongest days of the week?

Saturday and Sunday.
The rest are week days.

**What did the grape do
when he got stepped on?**

He let out a little wine.

**If you ever get cold,
just stand in a corner.**

They're usually 90 degrees.

**What did one eye say
to the other eye?**

Between you and me,
something smells.

Did you hear the joke about the roof?

Never mind, it's over your head.

**What did the hat
say to the hat rack?**

You stay here,
I'll go on ahead.

Why do vampires seem sick?

They're always coffin.

Why do geologists hate their jobs?

They get taken for granite.

**Did you hear the story about
the claustrophobic astronaut?**

He just needed some space.

**I decided to sell
my vacuum cleaner.**

It was just gathering dust.

I could tell a joke about pizza.

But it's a little cheesy.

What's an astronaut's favorite part of a keyboard?

The space bar.

Where do you learn all about ice cream?

Sundae school.

How do you weigh a millennial?

In Instagrams.

What happens when an artist has trouble finding inspiration?

He draws a blank.

I was going to tell a time-traveling joke, but you guys didn't like it.

I hate jokes about German sausages.

They're the wurst.

What lies at the bottom of the ocean and twitches?

A nervous wreck.

What did the drummer call his twin daughters?

Anna one, Anna two.

I wanted to go on a diet.

But I have way too much
on my plate right now.

**What do you call a bear
without any teeth?**

A gummy bear.

**I've never gone to
a gun range before.**

But I've decided to give it a shot.

Did you hear about the kidnapping at school?

It's fine, he woke up.

What did the caretaker say when he jumped out of the store cupboard?

'Supplies!'

When does a joke become a dad joke?

When it becomes apparent.

**Why is it hard to explain
puns to kleptomaniacs?**

They always take things literally.

**I'm thinking about
removing my spine.**

I feel like it's
holding me back.

**Do you think glass coffins
will be a success?**

Remains to be seen.

**Did you know that milk is
the fastest liquid on earth?**

It's pasteurized before
you even see it.

**Why are skeletons
so calm?**

Because nothing
gets under their skin.

**What kind of music do
the planets listen to?**

Nep-tunes.

Did you hear about the man who fell into an upholstery machine?

He's fully recovered.

I'll never date another apostrophe.

The last one was too possessive.

I gave all my dead batteries away today.

Free of charge.

I fear for the calendar.

It's days are numbered.

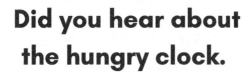

**Did you hear about
the hungry clock.**

It went back four seconds.

**An invisible man married
an invisable women.**

The kids are
nothing to look at.

I stayed up all night wondering where the sun went.

Then it dawned on me.

What do you call a seagull that flies over the bay?

A bagel.

I wasn't going to get a brain transplant.

Then I changed my mind.

Did you hear the story about the haunted lift?

It really raised my spirits.

The average person is really mean.

I asked my date to meet me at the gym, but she never showed up.

I guess the two of us aren't going to work out.

How do you get a country girl's attention?

A tractor.

Why are elevator jokes so good?

They work on many levels.

What do you call a pudgy psychic?

A four-chin teller.

**Why do nurses like
to carry crayons?**

Sometimes they have
to draw blood.

**My wife asked me get
6 cans of Sprite from
the grocery store.**

I realized when I got home
that I had picked 7 up.

Why do bees have sticky hair?

Because they use a honeycomb.

What's the most detail-oriented ocean?

The Pacific.

Why did the man fall down the well?

Because he couldn't see that well.

Sundays are always a little sad.

But the day before is a sadder day.

Why are frogs so happy?

They eat whatever bugs them.

I've been thinking about taking up meditation.

I figure it's better than sitting around doing nothing.

I lost my job at the bank on my first day. A woman asked me to check her balance.

So I pushed her over.

Singing in the shower is fun until you get soap in your mouth.

Then it becomes a soap opera.

I told my doctor I heard buzzing.

He said it's just a bug going around.

What kind of car does a sheep like to drive?

A lamborghini.

What did the accountant say while auditing a document?

This is taxing.

RIP boiled water.

You will be mist.

What do you call two octopuses that look the same?

Itenticle.

What does a house wear?

Address.

People are usually shocked that I have a Police record.

But I love their greatest hits.

Why shouldn't you write with a broken pencil?

Because it's pointless.

What's orange and sounds like a parrot?

A carrot.

Can one bird make a pun?

No, but toucan.

Why was the horse so happy?

Because he lived in
a stable environment.

**A termite walks into
a bar and says . . .**

"Where is the bar tender?"

**How do trees access
the internet?**

They log in.

**What is the best
Christmas present ever?**

A broken drum –
you can't beat it.

Made in the USA
Coppell, TX
15 September 2020

38075675R00059